SAMSUNG GALAXY S24 ULTRA
User Guide

*The Definitive teacher to Exploring
Innovation, Design Brilliance, and Camera
Mastery with Galaxy S24 Series*

Tech Talker

Table of contents

Introduction

Table of contents

Introduction

In the ever-evolving landscape of technology, the Galaxy S24 Series stands out as a testament to innovation, pushing the boundaries of what smartphones can achieve. This book delves into the intricacies of this cutting-edge series, exploring the profound impact of its innovative features, impeccable design, and state-of-the-art camera capabilities.

As we embark on this journey, it's essential to understand the role of innovation in shaping the modern smartphone experience. The Galaxy S24 Series serves as a beacon of progress, incorporating advanced technologies that redefine user expectations. From its unified design to the powerhouse of its camera system, every aspect is meticulously crafted to deliver an unparalleled mobile experience.

The significance of design excellence in smartphones cannot be overstated. The Galaxy S24 Series, with its unified design and satin finish, epitomizes elegance and ergonomics. As we explore the design brilliance of these devices, we uncover the seamless integration of form and function, providing users with a device that feels as smooth as it looks.

A pivotal focus of our exploration is the camera mastery embedded in the Galaxy S24 Series. In the era of visual communication, a smartphone's camera is its most influential feature. The series boasts a 50MP multi-camera system, Nightography capabilities, and AI-driven enhancements, empowering users to capture moments with unprecedented detail, clarity, and creativity.

The purpose of this book is to unravel the layers of innovation, design brilliance, and camera mastery within the Galaxy S24 Series. By delving into the intricacies of these features, we aim to provide readers with a comprehensive understanding of the technological marvel that is the Galaxy S24 Series. Whether you are an avid tech enthusiast, a smartphone photography enthusiast, or someone curious about the future of mobile technology, this book offers insights that transcend the conventional boundaries of smartphone literature. Join us as we navigate through the chapters, each revealing a facet of the Galaxy S24 Series that contributes to its status as a groundbreaking device in the realm of smartphones.

Chapter 1:

Unveiling the Galaxy S24 Series

In the world of smartphones, design is more than skin-deep. The Galaxy S24 and S24+ boast a unified design with a satin finish, creating a device that not only looks stunning but also feels smooth and comfortable in your hands. Join us as we unravel the design philosophy behind these devices, where form and function dance in perfect harmony.

In an era dominated by visual storytelling, the camera is the heart and soul of a smartphone. The Galaxy S24 and S24+ take mobile photography to unprecedented heights with a 50MP multi-camera system. Nightography capabilities ensure stunning shots in low light, while AI-driven enhancements add a touch of creativity to every capture. Join us in exploring the intricacies of the camera system that transforms every user into a photography enthusiast.

From the enhanced processing power to the immersive display experience, these devices redefine what's possible in the palm of your hand. We'll navigate through the features that make these devices a powerhouse, ensuring optimal performance, extended battery life, and a seamless transition from iOS.

As we embark on this exploration of the Galaxy S24 and S24+, our purpose is clear—to provide you, the reader, with an immersive understanding of these groundbreaking devices. Whether you're a tech enthusiast, a photography buff, or someone curious about the future of mobile technology, this journey is tailored to offer insights that transcend the conventional smartphone narrative.

Key features and specifications

The Galaxy S24 Series has emerged as a pinnacle of innovation, encapsulating cutting-edge features and specifications that redefine the smartphone experience. Let's delve into the key attributes that make these devices stand out:

Design Brilliance

The Galaxy S24 and S24+ boast a unified design, with a rounded back for enhanced grip and a satin finish that exudes sophistication. The use of improved Armor Aluminum not only enhances strength and hardness but also contributes to the devices' aesthetic appeal. The front and rear are fortified with Gorilla Glass Victus 2, ensuring durability and a sleek appearance.

Display

The devices feature stunning displays that elevate your visual experience. The Galaxy S24 sports a 6.2-inch FHD+ display, while the S24+ takes it a step further with a 6.7-inch QHD+ display. The Vision Booster technology optimizes color and contrast, ensuring optimal visibility even on bright days.

Camera Mastery

At the core of the Galaxy S24 Series is a camera system designed to capture moments with unparalleled clarity and detail. The 50MP multi-camera system, equipped with a 2x optical zoom, ensures high-resolution images that stand the test of time. Nightography capabilities extend to the front camera, delivering brilliant low-light selfies. The ProVisual engine enhances image quality, making every shot a masterpiece.

Galaxy AI Integration

Galaxy AI is the driving force behind an enriched mobile experience. From on-device features to cloud-based solutions, Galaxy AI permeates various aspects of the user interface. AI Zoom enhances the photography experience, Live Translate breaks down language barriers in real-time, and Chat Assist provides tone suggestions for professional and conversational writing.

Seamless Performance

Gaming enthusiasts will appreciate the larger Vapor Chamber, ensuring optimal heat dissipation and peak gaming performance. The devices come with 6.2" FHD+ and 6.7" QHD+ displays, offering more screen real estate. The intelligent battery management system extends game time, watch time, and personal time, making the Galaxy S24 Series your reliable companion throughout the day.

Connectivity and Sharing

Switching to Galaxy is seamless with Smart Switch, facilitating the effortless transfer of data from iOS or other Android devices. Quick Share enables instant sharing of photos, videos, and files, fostering efficient communication. The devices prioritize security with Knox and offer multi-device security for enhanced peace of mind.

Sustainability and Storage

In a commitment to a sustainable future, the Galaxy S24 Series takes small steps toward eco-friendliness. The devices come with ample storage options, ranging from 128GB to 512GB, ensuring that users can store their digital lives effortlessly.

The Galaxy S24 Series represents a convergence of innovation, design brilliance, and camera mastery, redefining the standards for smartphones. As we explore each facet in detail, the immersive experience these devices offer becomes increasingly evident. Join us on a journey through the intricacies of the Galaxy S24 and S24+, where every feature is a testament to the relentless pursuit of excellence in mobile technology.

Available colors

The Galaxy S24 Series not only excels in performance and features but also offers a diverse palette of colors to suit individual preferences.

Let's explore the captivating range of hues available for these exceptional devices:

1. **Cobalt Violet:** This vibrant shade adds a touch of elegance to your smartphone, making a bold statement with its deep and captivating tones.

2. **Amber Yellow:** Radiating warmth and energy, the Amber Yellow variant stands out as a lively and distinctive choice for those who appreciate a splash of color.

3. **Onyx Black:** A classic and timeless option, Onyx Black exudes sophistication and versatility, complementing any style with its sleek and polished appearance.

4. **Marble Gray:** Offering a balance between subtlety and modernity, Marble

Gray presents a refined and understated aesthetic, perfect for those who appreciate sophistication in simplicity.

5. **Jade Green:** Nature-inspired, Jade Green brings a refreshing and calming vibe, infusing a sense of tranquility into the device's visual appeal.

6. **Sapphire Blue:** Capturing the essence of deep blue waters, Sapphire Blue adds a touch of mystery and depth to the Galaxy S24 Series.

7. **Sandstone Orange:** Reflecting the warmth of the sun-kissed desert,

Sandstone Orange brings a unique and bold choice to the color palette.

These diverse color options not only allow users to express their personal style but also contribute to the overall aesthetics of the Galaxy S24 Series. Whether you prefer a timeless black, a vibrant pop of color, or an exclusive Samsung.com shade, the array of choices ensures that there's a Galaxy S24 for every taste.

Comparison with the previous Galaxy S23 Series

The Galaxy S24 Series introduces a refined design with a rounded back, providing a more comfortable grip. The unified design, featuring a satin finish for both the back glass and frame, adds a touch of sophistication. The Armor Aluminum construction has been improved for better strength and hardness. The front and rear boast Gorilla Glass Victus 2, ensuring durability and resilience against daily wear and tear.

One notable upgrade is the display size. The Galaxy S24 comes with a 6.2-inch FHD+ display, while the S24+ features a larger 6.7-inch QHD+ display. This not only offers more screen real estate for users but also provides an enhanced viewing experience. The Vision Booster technology optimizes color and contrast, ensuring optimal visibility even in bright outdoor conditions.

The camera capabilities have seen significant improvements. Both the Galaxy S24 and S24+ are equipped with a 12MP Selfie Camera and a triple Rear Camera setup. The 50MP Wide-angle Camera with 2x optical zoom, 12MP Ultra Wide Camera, and 10MP 3x Optical Zoom Camera collaborate to deliver stunning shots. Nightography, a feature dedicated to low-light photography, is now available on both the rear and selfie cameras, producing brilliant results even in challenging lighting conditions.

The introduction of the ProVisual engine enhances the detail and color reproduction in photos, ensuring vibrant and high-resolution images. This improvement is particularly noticeable in digital zoom distances, where the Galaxy S24 Series sets a new standard for clarity and sharpness.

Gaming enthusiasts will appreciate the larger Vapor Chamber in the Galaxy S24 Series, providing improved heat dissipation and maintaining peak gaming performance. The 6.2-inch FHD+ display on the Galaxy S24 and the 6.7-inch QHD+ display on the Galaxy S24+ offer an immersive gaming experience.

The intelligent battery in the Galaxy S24 and S24+ ensures extended usage time, allowing users to enjoy more game time, watch time, and personal time. With a focus on sustainability, these devices take small steps towards a greener future.

In summary, the Galaxy S24 Series builds upon the strengths of its predecessor, incorporating advancements in design, display, camera technology, performance, and battery efficiency. These enhancements collectively contribute to a smartphone experience that aligns with the ever-evolving needs of users in the digital age.

Chapter 2:

Design Brilliance

The unified design philosophy of the Galaxy S24 Series represents a harmonious blend of aesthetics and functionality. Samsung has meticulously crafted these devices, employing a design language that not only captivates the eye but also enhances the overall user experience.

At first glance, the Galaxy S24 and S24+ exude sophistication with their satin finish. The choice of materials and the meticulous crafting of the back glass and frame contribute to a seamless and elegant exterior. The satin finish not only adds a touch of luxury but also ensures a smooth and comfortable feel in hand.

One of the key elements of the unified design is the rounded back. This thoughtful design choice goes beyond aesthetics; it's a deliberate move to enhance the ergonomic aspect of the devices. The rounded back not only provides a comfortable grip but also contributes to a more natural and ergonomic feel during prolonged usage.

The Galaxy S24 Series introduces improved Armor Aluminum, reinforcing the structural integrity of the devices. This not only adds a layer of durability but also contributes to the sleek and unified appearance. The choice of materials reflects a commitment to both aesthetics and functionality.

Durability meets elegance with the implementation of Gorilla Glass Victus 2 on both the front and rear of the devices. This advanced glass technology not only provides robust protection against scratches and drops but also seamlessly integrates into the unified design, maintaining a cohesive and premium look.

The unified design philosophy extends across the spectrum of available colors. Whether it's Cobalt Violet, Amber Yellow, Onyx Black, or Marble Gray, each variant adheres to the same design principles. This consistency ensures that users can choose their preferred color without compromising the overall design integrity of the Galaxy S24 Series.

From the placement of buttons to the symmetry in design, every detail is meticulously considered. The unified design philosophy is not just about individual elements; it's about how these elements come together to create a holistic and visually pleasing device.

In essence, the unified design philosophy of the Galaxy S24 Series is a testament to Samsung's commitment to delivering smartphones that not only meet the highest standards of functionality but also stand out as objects of beauty. It's a design ethos that values both form and function, creating a device that seamlessly integrates into the user's lifestyle.

The Galaxy S24 and S24+ redefine the tactile and visual experience with their exquisite satin finish. Samsung has gone to great lengths to ensure that every interaction with these devices is not just functional but also a sensory delight.

The satin finish, meticulously applied to both the back glass and frame of the Galaxy S24 Series, contributes to a unified and luxurious aesthetic. This finish is not just a surface treatment but a design philosophy that elevates the overall look and feel of the devices.

Running your fingers across the Galaxy S24 or S24+ feels akin to gliding over silk. The satin finish imparts a smoothness that transcends the ordinary, making every touch a pleasurable experience. This is not just about aesthetics but about creating a tangible connection between the user and the device.

Beyond its visual appeal, the satin finish serves a practical purpose by enhancing the grip and comfort during usage. The rounded back, combined with the satin texture, ensures that the devices sit comfortably in the palm of your hand. This attention to detail is a nod to the importance of ergonomics in the design process.

The choice of a satin finish is a deliberate move towards a more refined and luxurious appearance. It adds a subtle sheen that catches the light in just the right way, creating an ever-changing visual experience. The Galaxy S24 and S24+ are not just smartphones; they are expressions of style and sophistication.

Despite the luxurious feel, the satin finish doesn't compromise on durability. The Galaxy S24 Series retains its resilience, resisting fingerprints and maintaining its pristine appearance over time. This balance between elegance and durability is a hallmark of Samsung's commitment to quality.

The satin finish goes beyond the visual and tactile—it's a sensory delight. It transforms the act of using a smartphone into a multisensory experience, where the feel of the device becomes an integral part of the overall satisfaction.

In essence, the satin finish of the Galaxy S24 and S24+ is a testament to Samsung's dedication to crafting devices that transcend utility and become objects of desire. It's a marriage of form and function, where the tactile experience is as important as the visual aesthetics, creating smartphones that are truly a pleasure to hold and behold.

Enhanced durability with Armor Aluminum

In the relentless pursuit of creating smartphones that not only boast cutting-edge technology but also stand the test of time, Samsung introduces a game-changing element to the Galaxy S24 and S24+—Armor Aluminum.

Armor Aluminum is not just a material; it's a philosophy that seeks to strike the perfect equilibrium between strength and elegance. Samsung engineers understand the pivotal role durability plays in the lifespan of a device, and Armor Aluminum is their answer to ensuring that the Galaxy S24 Series stands strong in the face of daily wear and tear.

The use of Armor Aluminum in crafting the frame of the Galaxy S24 and S24+ brings an unprecedented level of robustness. This aerospace-grade alloy is renowned for its exceptional strength-to-weight ratio, ensuring that your smartphone can withstand the rigors of daily life without adding unnecessary bulk.

Armor Aluminum goes beyond just providing physical strength; it is also resistant to corrosion and rust, enhancing the device's longevity. This feature is particularly crucial, considering the varied environments smartphones are exposed to, from humid climates to unexpected encounters with liquids.

One of the remarkable aspects of Armor Aluminum is its ability to maintain a slim and sleek design while offering unparalleled protection. The Galaxy S24 and S24+ epitomize the marriage of aesthetics and durability, proving that a robust smartphone doesn't have to compromise on elegance.

Accidental drops and impacts are inevitable aspects of a device's life. With Armor Aluminum, the Galaxy S24 Series adds an extra layer of defense against such incidents. The frame acts as a shield, mitigating the force of impacts and contributing to the overall structural integrity of the device.

Samsung's commitment to quality is embedded in every aspect of the Galaxy S24 and S24+, and Armor Aluminum exemplifies this dedication. The careful selection of materials and the meticulous manufacturing process underscore a commitment to delivering devices that not only meet but exceed user expectations.

In conclusion, the integration of Armor Aluminum in the Galaxy S24 and S24+ is a testament to Samsung's unwavering commitment to innovation, durability, and user satisfaction. It transforms these smartphones into not just devices but reliable companions that can weather the challenges of daily life while retaining their elegance and functionality.

User experience with the design

The design of a smartphone transcends mere aesthetics; it's an interaction, an experience, and in the case of the Galaxy S24 and S24+, it's a language that speaks to the user on a profound level. Samsung has carefully crafted these devices, ensuring that every curve, every finish, and every detail contributes to a seamless and delightful user experience.

From the moment you lay eyes on the Galaxy S24 and S24+, it becomes evident that a unified design philosophy guides every contour and detail. The rounded back, the precisely crafted frame, and the Gorilla Glass Victus on both front and rear—everything is orchestrated to provide a harmonious and cohesive visual appeal. This unity extends beyond aesthetics; it's a commitment to creating a device that feels like a singular, well-thought-out entity.

The Galaxy S24 Series introduces a satin finish to both the back glass and the frame. This isn't just about looks; it's about tactile pleasure. The smoothness of the satin finish creates an exquisite feel, turning the act of holding your smartphone into an experience. It's a touch of luxury that enhances the overall user satisfaction, making every interaction with the device a moment of delight.

Samsung understands that personal expression matters. The Galaxy S24 and S24+ come in a palette of colors, including Cobalt Violet, Amber Yellow, Onyx Black, and Marble Gray. Exclusive colors like Jade Green, Sapphire Blue, and Sandstone Orange available only on Samsung.com offer users the opportunity to choose a device that not only suits their technological needs but also aligns with their style and personality.

Despite the array of features packed into the Galaxy S24 and S24+, the slim design ensures that the devices don't just fit comfortably in your hand but also seamlessly integrate into your lifestyle. The slim profile doesn't compromise on structural integrity, thanks to the innovative use of Armor Aluminum, offering durability without sacrificing elegance.

The front and rear of the Galaxy S24 Series are fortified with Gorilla Glass Victus 2, adding an extra layer of protection. This not only contributes to the device's durability but also ensures that the display remains vivid and crystal clear. The display becomes a window into the digital realm, inviting users to immerse themselves fully in the content.

In essence, the user experience with the design of the Galaxy S24 and S24+ is one of cohesion, elegance, and thoughtful innovation. Every element is a piece of a larger puzzle, carefully designed to resonate with users on both a visual and tactile level. It's not just a smartphone; it's an extension of your style, a companion that understands and enhances your daily experiences.

Chapter 3:
Camera Mastery

In the fast-paced world we live in, a smartphone's camera is more than just a feature; it's a portal to our memories, a tool for creative expression, and a means to connect with the world visually.

The Galaxy S24 Series understands this dynamic and introduces a camera system that goes beyond specifications, aiming to redefine how we perceive and capture the moments that matter.

Triple Rear Camera System:

At the heart of the Galaxy S24 and S24+ lies a sophisticated triple rear camera system. This system is not just about numbers; it's about versatility and performance. The 50MP wide-angle camera serves as the powerhouse, ensuring that every shot is rich in detail and clarity. Complemented by the 12MP ultra-wide camera and the 10MP 3x optical zoom camera, users have a comprehensive toolkit for capturing a wide range of scenes with varying perspectives.

Nightography for Low-Light Brilliance:

The Galaxy S24 Series takes a significant leap in low-light photography with Nightography. This feature isn't restricted to the rear camera alone; it extends its brilliance to the 12MP selfie camera as well.

Now, capturing stunning shots in dimly lit environments is not just a possibility but a delightful reality. The dedicated ISP Block and ProVisual engine ensure that even in challenging lighting conditions, your photos and videos retain vibrancy, reduced noise, and enhanced detail.

AI-Powered Zoom for Every Detail:

Zooming in on your subjects without compromising quality is a hallmark of the Galaxy S24 camera system.

The AI-powered zoom functionality keeps pictures crisp, clear, and super sharp, whether you're at 1x, 2x, or 3x zoom. This isn't just about getting closer to your subjects; it's about preserving the essence of the moment with exceptional clarity.

Super HDR: A Window to True-to-Life Colors:

Super HDR on the Galaxy S24 ensures that what you see in the preview is what you get in the final shot. The ability to preview HDR quality before capturing the image is a game-changer, providing users with confidence in their shots. Whether you're a photography enthusiast or a casual shooter, Super HDR makes every photo a masterpiece.

Generative Edit: Unleashing the Power of AI in Editing:

Beyond capturing moments, the Galaxy S24 camera system brings the power of AI to the realm of editing. Generative Edit is a revolutionary feature that fills in backgrounds, removes unwanted objects, and adds a touch of magic to your photos.

Resize it, retouch it. Just like that

Rotate your photo and let background fill complete the missing corners to fit the frame.²

Select and move an object in your photo and AI will fill in the space it leaves behind like it was never there.³

It's not just about capturing reality; it's about creating the ideal visual narrative with every shot.

The camera system of the Galaxy S24 and S24+ is a testament to Samsung's commitment to empowering users with a tool that goes beyond traditional photography. It's a creative companion, a low-light maestro, and a guardian of true-to-life colors. With the Galaxy S24 Series, every click is an opportunity to tell your story visually, with unparalleled detail and brilliance.

Chapter 4:
Galaxy AI Features

In the ever-evolving landscape of technology, the Galaxy S24 Series stands at the forefront of innovation, and at the heart of this technological marvel lies the transformative power of Galaxy AI. More than just a set of features, Galaxy AI represents a paradigm shift in the way we interact with our smartphones, transcending conventional boundaries and ushering in a new era of mobile experiences.

Galaxy AI is not a mere addition to the Galaxy S24; it's a holistic transformation, an amalgamation of on-device and cloud-based AI solutions designed to elevate every facet of user experience. It's a symphony of productivity, creativity, and play, where every interaction with your smartphone becomes an intelligent, seamless, and anticipatory journey.

One of the standout arenas where Galaxy AI flexes its muscles is in the camera system. AI Zoom redefines the boundaries of zoom photography, ensuring that every shot, from wide-angle vistas to close-up details, is captured with precision and clarity. Nightography, powered by AI, extends its brilliance to low-light scenarios, making every dimly lit moment an opportunity for stunning visuals.

Editing photos becomes a breeze with Generative Edit, an AI-powered feature that fills in backgrounds, removes unwanted elements, and transforms your photos into artistic masterpieces. The magic of AI isn't just in capturing moments but in enhancing and shaping them to match your creative vision.

Communication knows no bounds with Live Translate. Real-time language translations during calls or texts open up a world of possibilities, making conversations seamless and eliminating language barriers. It's not just a translation tool; it's a bridge that connects individuals across languages.

Circle to Search introduces a novel way of interacting with the world through your camera. Simply circle an object, and Galaxy AI will fetch relevant Google Search results. It's a visual search experience that adds a layer of convenience and exploration to your everyday interactions.

Enhance your written communication with Chat Assist. Receive real-time tone suggestions to strike the right balance between professionalism and conversational flair. It's not just a writing tool; it's a companion that helps you put your best text forward.

As we unravel the layers of Galaxy AI within the Galaxy S24 Series, it becomes evident that we're not just witnessing an incremental upgrade; we're stepping into a new frontier of possibilities. Galaxy AI is the silent, intelligent force that turns every interaction into an experience, making the Galaxy S24 Series more than a smartphone—it's a glimpse into the future of mobile technology.

On-device and cloud-based AI solutions

In the intricate dance of technological evolution, the synergy between on-device and cloud-based AI solutions within the Galaxy S24 Series orchestrates a symphony of seamless, intelligent experiences. It's not just about the raw power of processing; it's about finding the delicate balance that ensures efficiency, privacy, and a user experience that transcends expectations.

The Galaxy S24 Series leverages the power of on-device AI to handle tasks directly within the smartphone itself. This on-device processing is not just a matter of convenience; it's a strategic move to enhance speed, responsiveness, and data privacy. From translating languages in real-time during calls with Live Translate to crafting intelligent suggestions in Chat Assist, on-device AI is the silent force that empowers your smartphone to be a smart companion.

While on-device AI handles local tasks swiftly, the inclusion of cloud-based AI solutions broadens the scope of possibilities. Leveraging the immense computational power of the cloud, certain features seamlessly integrate global databases, ensuring accurate and up-to-date information. Features like Circle to Search, with its intricate web of visual recognition and Google Search results, showcase the prowess of cloud-based AI in enhancing our exploration of the world through the smartphone lens.

What makes the Galaxy S24 Series truly remarkable is the orchestration of on-device and cloud-based AI solutions into a unified, cohesive experience. It's not a mere juxtaposition of technologies; it's a conscious design choice aimed at providing users with the best of both worlds. The device becomes an extension of your intelligence, with on-device AI handling swift, personalized tasks and cloud-based AI expanding the horizons of what your smartphone can achieve.

As we traverse the landscape of AI, privacy remains a paramount concern. The Galaxy S24 Series prioritizes user privacy by ensuring that sensitive tasks are handled on-device, minimizing the need to transmit personal data to the cloud. It's a delicate dance between the power of the cloud and the intimacy of on-device processing, ensuring that your smartphone remains your personal sanctuary.

In the intricate interplay of on-device and cloud-based AI, the Galaxy S24 Series not only redefines what a smartphone can do but also exemplifies a commitment to a user-centric, intelligent future. It's not just about processing power; it's about crafting a harmonious symphony of intelligence that enhances every facet of the user experience.

Live Translate: Breaking language barriers in real-time

In a world where communication knows no borders, the Galaxy S24 Series introduces Live Translate, a groundbreaking feature that transcends language barriers, fostering real-time conversations that are as fluid as the thoughts they convey. It's not just a tool; it's a bridge that brings people closer, no matter the languages they speak.

Live Translate is your linguistic companion, making conversations with people who speak different languages a breeze. Picture this: you're in a foreign country, needing to communicate with a taxi driver to navigate the bustling streets. With Live Translate, you simply make the call, and as the conversation unfolds, the spoken words transform into a text conversation on your screen, providing real-time translations in both languages. It's not just translation; it's a seamless exchange of ideas.

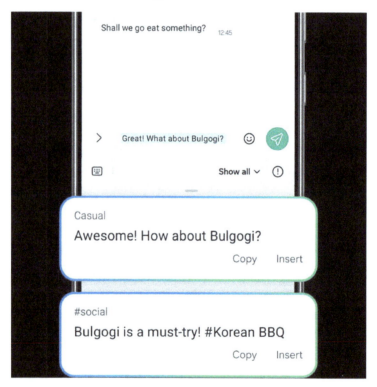

How It Works:

Activating Live Translate is as intuitive as the conversations it facilitates. A simple tap on the Phone app leads you to a world where language is no longer a barrier. Once in the app, a few straightforward steps are all it takes to enable Live Translate. Choose your languages, set preferences for translated voices, and embark on a journey where communication transcends linguistic confines.

Live Translate extends its prowess beyond phone calls, seamlessly integrating into various aspects of your digital interactions. Whether you're exchanging messages, browsing social feeds, or watching videos, Live Translate is there to break down language barriers. Need to decipher a text in a social media image post? Circle it on-screen, and Live Translate seamlessly connects the object to a Google Search result page, providing instant information.

Customization is key, and Live Translate understands that. Tailor the experience to your liking by choosing from a selection of translated voices and adjusting speech rates. It's not just about understanding words; it's about capturing the nuances of communication, ensuring that every conversation feels natural and authentic.

Live Translate is not just a feature; it's a testament to the transformative power of technology in fostering global connections. Breaking language barriers in real-time, it opens doors to new friendships, smoother travel experiences, and a world where understanding knows no bounds. The Galaxy S24 Series, with Live Translate at its core, redefines how we communicate, making every conversation a celebration of diversity and shared understanding.

Chat Assist: Real-time tone suggestions for professional or conversational writing

Introducing Chat Assist, a revolutionary tool embedded in the Galaxy S24 Series that goes beyond autocorrect and predictive text. It's your personal writing companion, offering real-time tone suggestions to ensure your messages strike the perfect balance between professionalism and conversational flair. With Chat Assist, your words resonate exactly as you intend, making every written interaction a polished and impactful experience.

In the fast-paced digital age, the way we communicate matters more than ever. Chat Assist steps in as your co-pilot in the realm of text, ensuring that your written expressions align with the tone you wish to convey. Whether you're drafting a business email, composing a heartfelt message, or engaging in casual chats, Chat Assist tailors its suggestions to suit the context and mood.

How It Works:

Chat Assist seamlessly integrates into your text input, offering unobtrusive suggestions that appear as you type. It analyzes the tone of your message and provides alternatives, allowing you to choose the one that best aligns with your communication style. It's not about changing your voice; it's about refining it, ensuring that your words leave a lasting impact.

For business professionals, Chat Assist is a game-changer. Need to draft a formal email that exudes professionalism? Let Chat Assist guide you with suggestions that elevate your language without compromising authenticity. It understands the nuances of business communication, helping you navigate the fine line between formality and approachability.

On the flip side, Chat Assist is equally adept at infusing a touch of charm into your casual conversations. Whether you're catching up with friends or engaging in social banter, it suggests expressions that add flair and personality to your messages. It's the secret ingredient that turns ordinary texts into memorable exchanges.

One size doesn't fit all, and Chat Assist understands that. Tailor its suggestions to match your unique writing style by adjusting the settings to your preferences. It's not just a tool; it's a personalized writing coach that adapts to your needs, making your written communication as distinctive as you are.

Chat Assist doesn't just correct; it collaborates. From professional emails to casual chats, it's there to refine your tone, ensuring that every word reflects your intent. With Chat Assist on your Galaxy S24, your writing becomes a dynamic, expressive canvas, leaving a lasting impression in every message you convey.

Circle to Search: A new way to search with a circle gesture

Introducing Circle to Search, a cutting-edge feature on the Galaxy S24 Series that transcends traditional search methods.

This innovative functionality lets you seamlessly transition from the physical world to the digital realm with a simple and intuitive circular gesture. Say goodbye to traditional typing and tapping; with Circle to Search, you can effortlessly discover information in a way that feels natural and engaging.

How Circle to Search Works:

Imagine you come across an intriguing object in a social media image or real life. Instead of typing out a search query, you can now use Circle to Search. Simply draw a circle around the object on your screen, and like magic, the Galaxy S24 interprets your gesture and initiates a Google Search related to that object.

In Social Media:

Circle to Search transforms the way you interact with social media. If you spot a captivating image or post featuring something you want to learn more about, just circle it. The Galaxy S24 instantly connects your gesture to a Google Search, providing you with relevant information without interrupting your social media experience.

In Messages:

Text messages often spark curiosity about various topics. With Circle to Search, you can seamlessly transition from a text conversation to an informative search. If a friend mentions a place, an event, or anything that piques your interest, circle it within the chat, and relevant Google Search results appear at your fingertips.

In Videos:

Watching videos and come across something intriguing? Circle to Search brings a new dimension to video interaction. If you see an item you'd like to explore further in a video, perform the circle gesture. The Galaxy S24 initiates a Google Search related to the circled item, letting you seamlessly merge your video-watching and information-gathering experiences.

Effortless Exploration:

Circle to Search is designed to make information discovery effortless. No more pausing to type out queries or switching between apps. This feature streamlines your exploration process, allowing you to effortlessly bridge the physical and digital worlds with a simple circular motion.

Customized for Your Convenience:
Circle to Search is adaptable to various scenarios. Whether you're exploring social media, decoding text messages, or delving into video content, the Galaxy S24 tailors its search capabilities to your context. It's a dynamic tool that aligns with your needs, making information retrieval a seamless and engaging experience.

With Circle to Search, the Galaxy S24 Series invites you to explore the digital realm in an entirely new way. Embrace the power of a simple circle gesture, connecting your curiosity to a wealth of information without missing a beat. It's more than a feature; it's a transformative bridge between the physical and digital, empowering you to explore effortlessly.

Transcript Assist: Real-time suggestions for text messages

Texting is an integral part of modern communication, and Transcript Assist aims to make it more seamless than ever.

As you compose your messages, this feature provides instant tone suggestions, helping you craft texts that resonate with your intended style. It's like having a personal writing assistant right at your fingertips.

How Transcript Assist Works:

Picture this: you're typing out a message, and you want it to convey a specific tone—perhaps professional, casual, or friendly. With Transcript Assist, you don't have to second-guess your wording. As you type, the Galaxy S24 analyzes your text in real-time and offers suggestions to align with your desired tone.

For business-related messages or formal communication, Transcript Assist ensures that your texts maintain a polished and professional demeanor. It recognizes key elements in your message and suggests enhancements that elevate the overall tone, making your communication more impactful.

On the flip side, when you're engaging in casual conversations with friends or family, Transcript Assist adapts to bring out the conversational flair. It understands the context of your messages and suggests wording that adds a touch of friendliness or warmth, creating a more natural flow.

Transcript Assist is not a one-size-fits-all solution. It adapts to your unique style of writing. Whether you prefer concise and to the point or expressive and detailed, this feature aligns with your individual preferences, ensuring that your texts feel authentically yours.

Say goodbye to the time-consuming process of meticulously choosing each word. Transcript Assist streamlines your writing experience, allowing you to focus on the message itself rather than getting caught up in the details. It's a tool designed to enhance efficiency without compromising on personalization.

AI-powered photo editing with Generative Edit

Unleash the power of AI in transforming your photos with Generative Edit, a groundbreaking feature on the Galaxy S24 Series. Bid farewell to conventional photo editing hassles as this cutting-edge tool revolutionizes the way you retouch and enhance your images. Let's delve into the world of Generative Edit and discover how it brings a touch of magic to your photography journey.

Seamless Background Fills:

Ever had a perfect photo ruined by distracting elements at the corners or edges? Generative Edit swoops in to save the day. As you edit your photos in the Gallery app, this AI-driven feature seamlessly fills in background areas, completing missing corners and ensuring your images fit the frame flawlessly. It's like having a virtual artist perfecting your compositions.

Object Resizing and Moving:

Do you wish you could rearrange the elements in your photos effortlessly? Generative Edit makes it happen. Simply select an object within your photo, and watch as the AI smoothly resizes and relocates it to another part of the image. The missing areas are magically filled in, creating a cohesive and visually pleasing composition.

The Magic Touch:

Generative Edit isn't just about fixing imperfections; it's about adding that extra touch of magic to your photos. Whether it's adjusting the composition, resizing elements, or filling in missing details, this feature ensures that your images look not just edited but professionally curated. It's the magic wand your photos have been waiting for.

AI-Powered Precision:

The beauty of Generative Edit lies in its precision. The AI algorithms analyze your photo's structure, understand the relationships between elements, and execute edits with accuracy. Say goodbye to manual, time-consuming adjustments—Generative Edit takes care of the details so you can focus on the artistry.

Unlocking Creativity:

Photography is an art form, and Generative Edit aims to unlock your creative potential. Experiment with different compositions, rearrange elements, and explore new dimensions in your photos. The AI's ability to fill in missing areas seamlessly allows you to push the boundaries of conventional editing, giving your images a distinctive flair.

Effortless Editing Workflow:

Generative Edit seamlessly integrates into your photo editing workflow, ensuring that the process is not just efficient but also enjoyable. The intuitive controls, coupled with the AI's ability to understand your editing intent, make it easy for both beginners and seasoned photographers to enhance their images effortlessly.

With Generative Edit, the Galaxy S24 Series invites you to elevate your photography experience. Embrace the future of photo editing, where AI-driven magic transforms your images into masterpieces. Whether you're a casual photographer or a seasoned pro, Generative Edit is your gateway to a new realm of creative possibilities.

Chapter 5:

Performance and Gaming

Embark on a gaming journey like never before with the Galaxy S24 Series, equipped with the revolutionary Vapor Chamber technology. Designed to push the boundaries of gaming performance, this cutting-edge feature ensures optimal cooling and unleashes the full potential of your device. Let's dive into the realm of Vapor Chamber and explore how it transforms your gaming experience into a seamless and exhilarating adventure.

PERFORMANCE

Game on with a larger Vapor Chamber

The Vapor Chamber on the Galaxy S24 Series isn't just an incremental improvement—it's a game-changer. Sized over 1.5 times larger than its predecessor, this advanced cooling system takes smartphone gaming to new heights. As you delve into intense gaming sessions, the Vapor Chamber efficiently dissipates heat, ensuring that your device stays cool even during the most demanding scenarios.

Gaming is not just a pastime; it's an immersive experience that demands peak performance. The enhanced Vapor Chamber on the Galaxy S24 Series guarantees optimal temperature management, preventing overheating and maintaining the device's performance at its zenith. Say goodbye to lags, stutters, and disruptions—immerse yourself in gaming nirvana.

While the Vapor Chamber delivers unparalleled cooling capabilities, it does so with a commitment to silence. Experience the power of efficient cooling without the unnecessary fan noise. The Galaxy S24 Series ensures a quiet and focused gaming environment, allowing you to get lost in the virtual worlds without distractions.

Picture this: you're in the midst of an action-packed gaming sequence, your device rendering graphics seamlessly, and the Vapor Chamber silently ensuring that the temperature remains optimal. Whether you're battling foes, exploring vast landscapes, or engaging in multiplayer showdowns, the Vapor Chamber is your silent ally, guaranteeing a smooth and uninterrupted gaming experience.

The Galaxy S24 Series, fortified by Vapor Chamber technology, invites you to break free from limitations. Push your gaming boundaries, explore graphic-intensive titles, and indulge in the adrenaline rush of competitive gaming. The device adapts to your gaming ambitions, ensuring that every tap, swipe, and action is met with responsiveness and precision.

With Vapor Chamber at its core, the Galaxy S24 Series is not just a smartphone; it's a gaming powerhouse. Elevate your gaming standards, embrace the future of mobile gaming, and let the Vapor Chamber redefine your expectations. Get ready for a gaming experience that's cool, silent, and unparalleled—just as it should be.

Larger Vapor Chamber on the Galaxy S24 Series

The Galaxy S24 Series redefines performance with an enhanced Vapor Chamber, showcasing a significant upgrade that goes beyond the ordinary.

The Vapor Chamber on the Galaxy S24 Series is not just a routine component—it's a technological marvel that has undergone a substantial size augmentation. Measuring over 1.5 times larger than its predecessor, this Vapor Chamber is a testament to Samsung's commitment to pushing the boundaries of mobile technology. Its expanded dimensions play a pivotal role in enhancing the overall performance of the devices, especially during resource-intensive tasks like gaming.

One of the primary functions of the Vapor Chamber is to manage the thermal dynamics of the device effectively. As smartphones continue to evolve into powerful computing devices, they generate more heat during demanding activities. The larger Vapor Chamber addresses this challenge by providing a more expansive surface area for heat dissipation. This translates to improved thermal management, preventing the device from overheating and ensuring sustained high performance.

Whether you are engaged in gaming marathons, video editing, or multitasking with resource-heavy applications, the larger Vapor Chamber ensures that the Galaxy S24 Series remains cool under pressure. It actively dissipates heat, allowing you to push the limits of your device without compromising on performance. This optimal cooling mechanism is designed to deliver a seamless and responsive user experience, irrespective of the complexity of the task at hand.

Efficiency and silence go hand in hand with the larger Vapor Chamber. While it excels in maintaining optimal temperatures, it does so without introducing unnecessary noise into the equation. This is particularly advantageous for gamers who seek an immersive and distraction-free environment. The Galaxy S24 Series, fortified by the larger Vapor Chamber, lets you enjoy your gaming sessions in tranquility, ensuring that the only sounds you hear are the ones crafted by the game itself.

As mobile technology continues to advance, the larger Vapor Chamber positions the Galaxy S24 Series as a device that's ready for the future. It acknowledges the increasing demands placed on smartphones and proactively addresses the challenges associated with heat dissipation. This forward-looking approach ensures that users can explore the full potential of their devices without being hindered by thermal limitations.

The larger Vapor Chamber on the Galaxy S24 Series is not merely a feature; it's a testament to Samsung's dedication to delivering devices that redefine user expectations. In the next chapter, we will explore how this advanced cooling technology specifically enhances gaming performance, showcasing its real-world impact on the user experience. Get ready to witness the Galaxy S24 Series in action, where every tap and swipe is powered by the efficiency of the larger Vapor Chamber.

Display sizes and improvements on Galaxy S24 and S24+

In the ever-evolving landscape of smartphones, the display is a crucial element that defines the user experience. The Galaxy S24 and S24+ stand at the forefront of innovation, boasting larger and more impressive displays that elevate your interactions with the digital world. In this chapter, we embark on a journey to explore the immersive display sizes and the noteworthy improvements that make these devices visual powerhouses.

The Galaxy S24 Series introduces larger displays, enriching your visual experience and redefining the way you engage with content. The Galaxy S24 features a 6.2-inch

FHD+ display, while the Galaxy S24+ takes it a step further with a 6.7-inch QHD+ display. These expanded screen sizes open up new possibilities for productivity, entertainment, and creativity, providing more real estate for your ideas and content to come to life.

The advancements in display technology extend beyond size, with the introduction of Vision Booster technology. Designed to optimize color and contrast, Vision Booster ensures that the Galaxy S24 Series displays deliver vibrant and true-to-life visuals even in challenging lighting conditions. Whether you're outdoors on a bright day or immersed in content during the night, Vision Booster enhances visibility, allowing you to appreciate every detail.

The Galaxy S24 and S24+ displays are not just larger; they also offer an extended canvas for your creativity and productivity. The increased screen real estate is particularly beneficial for multitasking, enabling you to run multiple applications simultaneously without compromising on usability. This expansive viewing canvas empowers you to effortlessly navigate through your digital world, enhancing efficiency and user satisfaction.

To further enrich your daily interactions, the Galaxy S24 Series introduces customizable widgets on the lock screen and Always On Display. These widgets provide at-a-glance information, from weather updates to your local air quality, ensuring that your device becomes a personalized hub of relevant and timely data.

As we immerse ourselves in the visual wonders of the Galaxy S24 and S24+ displays, it becomes evident that Samsung has meticulously crafted these devices to deliver an unparalleled viewing experience.

Vision Booster: Optimal color and contrast even in bright conditions

In the pursuit of creating a display that goes beyond expectations, Samsung introduces Vision Booster technology in the Galaxy S24 Series. This revolutionary feature is designed to optimize color and contrast, ensuring that your viewing experience remains exceptional even in the brightest conditions. Join us as we delve into the significance of Vision Booster, understanding how it transforms your interaction with the Galaxy S24 and S24+ displays.

One of the persistent challenges in smartphone displays is maintaining optimal visibility in bright outdoor environments. Whether you're checking your phone under direct sunlight or navigating through content in well-lit surroundings, the screen's visibility can be compromised. This challenge has fueled the need for innovative solutions that can adapt to varying lighting conditions without sacrificing visual quality.

Vision Booster is Samsung's answer to the challenge of bright conditions. It is a dynamic technology integrated into the display system of the Galaxy S24 Series, with a primary goal of enhancing color vibrancy and contrast. By intelligently adjusting parameters in real-time, Vision Booster ensures that your screen remains vivid and clear, regardless of external lighting factors. This means you can enjoy optimal color reproduction and detailed visuals even in the sunniest of days.

What sets Vision Booster apart is its adaptability. The technology doesn't rely on fixed settings but rather continuously analyzes the ambient lighting conditions. Based on this analysis, Vision Booster dynamically adjusts the color profiles and contrast levels to provide an optimal viewing experience. The result is a display that automatically tailors itself to the specific lighting scenario, delivering a consistently brilliant and immersive visual experience.

While Vision Booster excels in bright outdoor environments, its benefits extend beyond sunny days. The technology also contributes to enhancing visibility in various lighting conditions, including indoor settings with intense artificial lighting. This adaptability ensures that your Galaxy S24 or S24+ display remains a visual powerhouse across different scenarios, allowing you to appreciate the full spectrum of colors and details in your content.

Customization with widgets on the lock screen and Always On Display

Immerse yourself in a new realm of customization with the Galaxy S24 Series, where widgets seamlessly integrate into your lock screen and Always On Display (AOD). In this chapter, we'll explore the art of personalization, showcasing how widgets elevate your daily experience by providing at-a-glance access to essential information. Let's delve into the intuitive world of widgets, where convenience meets individuality.

Unlock the potential of your lock screen by adding widgets that offer real-time information without unlocking your device. Weather updates, calendar events, and quick access to your music player – these are just a glimpse of what lock screen widgets bring to your fingertips.

Imagine glancing at your phone and instantly knowing the weather forecast for the day or having a visual representation of your upcoming appointments. With lock screen widgets, you have the power to tailor your lock screen to reflect the information that matters most to you.

Extend the customization to the Always On Display, a feature that keeps your screen minimally active to showcase essential information when your device is not in use. Now, imagine having widgets on this ambient display, providing valuable insights into your day even before unlocking your phone.

From moon phases to air quality, and even a visual representation of your connected device battery status – the possibilities are vast. Widgets on AOD transform your idle screen into a canvas of personalized information, making every glance at your phone a delightful and informative experience.

The beauty of widgets lies in their adaptability. You have the flexibility to choose and arrange widgets based on your preferences. Whether you're a weather enthusiast, a music lover, or someone keen on tracking daily activities, there's a widget to cater to your needs.

Customization doesn't stop at choosing widgets; you can also arrange and resize them to create a layout that aligns with your aesthetic taste. This level of personalization ensures that your Galaxy S24 or S24+ becomes an extension of your personality, offering a user interface that resonates with your lifestyle.

Lock screen and AOD widgets aren't just about aesthetics – they contribute to your daily efficiency. With quick access to pertinent information, you can stay informed and organized, streamlining your interactions with the device. Whether you're on the move or in a meeting, widgets empower you to navigate through your day with ease.

Chapter 6:
All-Day Battery and Daily Experience

Embark on a journey where power meets intelligence with the Galaxy S24 Series. In this chapter, we delve into the intricacies of the intelligent battery features, designed to seamlessly align with your usage patterns and ensure your device remains a reliable companion throughout the day. Let's explore how the Galaxy S24 and S24+ redefine power management, making every charge count.

The heart of the intelligent battery lies in its adaptability. The Galaxy S24 Series employs advanced algorithms to understand and learn your usage patterns. Over time, the device optimizes power distribution, ensuring that energy is directed where it's needed most based on your daily activities.

Whether you're engrossed in a gaming marathon, capturing memories with the impressive camera system, or simply navigating your day with productivity apps, the intelligent battery intuitively adjusts its performance to provide an optimal balance between power efficiency and functionality.

A device that keeps up with your lifestyle – that's the promise of the Galaxy S24 Series. With an intelligent battery that extends the boundaries, you can enjoy more game time, watch time, and, most importantly, you time. Revel in the immersive gaming experiences, binge-watch your favorite shows, and stay connected without constantly worrying about running out of battery.

The Galaxy S24 and S24+ set new standards, offering up to 28 hours of video playback on the Galaxy S24 and 29 hours on the Galaxy S24+. When it comes to music, enjoy up to 72 hours on the Galaxy S24 and a staggering 88 hours on the Galaxy S24+. This extended battery life ensures that your device is ready to accompany you through the various facets of your day.

Switching to a new device should be effortless, and the Galaxy S24 Series ensures just that with Smart Switch. Whether you are transitioning from an iOS device or another Android, Smart Switch facilitates the transfer of your photos, contacts, calendar, and apps. Even as you upgrade to the latest Galaxy device, the intelligent battery management seamlessly integrates with your data, maintaining the same power efficiency.

Beyond immediate power management, the Galaxy S24 Series takes a step towards a sustainable future. With an understanding that every small change contributes to a larger impact, the device is designed to encourage sustainable practices. As we continue our exploration, we'll dive deeper into the eco-friendly initiatives and the role the Galaxy S24 Series plays in shaping a greener tomorrow.

Extended watch time, game time, and overall usage

The device introduces an extended watch time that allows you to indulge in your favorite movies, TV shows, and videos for prolonged durations without the worry of running out of battery.

On the Galaxy S24, enjoy an impressive 28 hours of video playback, while the Galaxy S24+ takes it even further with a remarkable 29 hours. This extended watch time ensures that you can binge-watch entire seasons, catch up on the latest releases, or simply unwind with your preferred content without the need for constant recharging.

Gaming enthusiasts, rejoice! The Galaxy S24 Series is engineered to deliver an exhilarating gaming experience with extended game time. Whether you're immersed in action-packed adventures, strategic battles, or multiplayer showdowns, the device ensures that your gaming sessions are not cut short by battery limitations.

The innovative Vapor Chamber technology, coupled with an intelligent battery management system, allows you to push the boundaries of gaming on your Galaxy S24 or S24+. With over 72 hours of music playback on the Galaxy S24 and an astounding 88 hours on the Galaxy S24+, your device becomes a gaming hub that adapts to your playstyle, offering extended entertainment without compromise.

Beyond specific activities like watching videos or playing games, the Galaxy S24 Series extends its capabilities for overall usage. The intelligent battery, optimized power management, and enhanced durability ensure that your device is ready for whatever the day throws at you.

Navigate through productivity tasks, communicate seamlessly, capture memories with the advanced camera system, and stay connected without the constant need to recharge. The Galaxy S24 and S24+ are designed to align with your dynamic lifestyle, offering extended usage that complements your digital journey.

Always On Display options

The Always On Display (AOD) on the Galaxy S24 Series offers a range of customizable options to enhance user experience. Whether you want to stay informed about the weather, monitor your daily schedule, or enjoy a personalized touch, the AOD provides a convenient and visually appealing way to interact with your device.

The AOD allows you to add widgets that provide at-a-glance information. These widgets can include the current weather, moon phase, air quality, and connected device battery status. Tailor your AOD to suit your preferences and keep the information you find most relevant readily available.

For music enthusiasts, the AOD includes a music player control panel. Easily access playback controls, track information, and adjust volume without unlocking your device. It's a seamless way to manage your music experience on the go.

The transition from the lock screen to the AOD is smooth and intuitive. Widgets displayed on the AOD mirror those you've set on your lock screen, providing consistency and quick access to essential information.

Choose from various AOD styles to match your personal taste. Whether you prefer a minimalist clock or a more elaborate design, the AOD allows you to express your style and customize your device's look and feel.

Stay in the loop with dynamic updates on your AOD. Receive notifications, check the time, and view important information without fully waking up your device. The AOD ensures that essential details are just a glance away.

Despite its informative features, the AOD is designed to be energy-efficient. It intelligently conserves battery life by displaying only essential information, ensuring that your device stays powered throughout the day.

The Always On Display on the Galaxy S24 Series is a versatile and user-friendly feature that seamlessly integrates into your daily routine, providing both style and functionality at a glance.

Seamless switch from iOS with Smart Switch

Making the switch from iOS to the Galaxy S24 Series is a hassle-free experience, thanks to the Smart Switch feature. Whether you're upgrading to a new device or transitioning from an iPhone, Smart Switch ensures that you can seamlessly transfer your important data, ensuring a smooth transition.

Move data from different OS | Switch through many ways | Switch various types of data

Smart Switch simplifies the process of moving your contacts, photos, messages, and more from your iOS device to your new Galaxy S24. With just a few taps, you can initiate the transfer and let Smart Switch handle the rest.

No need to worry about leaving important information behind. Smart Switch is designed to transfer a wide range of data, including contacts, calendar events, photos, videos, messages, and even your favorite apps. This ensures that you can pick up right where you left off on your new Galaxy device.

The Smart Switch interface is intuitive and user-friendly, guiding you through the transfer process step by step. Whether you're a tech enthusiast or a casual user,

Smart Switch makes the migration process accessible to everyone.

Choose the method that suits you best. Smart Switch supports both wired and wireless transfers, providing flexibility based on your preferences and the resources available to you. Connect your devices via a USB cable or use wireless connectivity for added convenience.

Once the transfer is complete, you'll find that your Galaxy S24 mirrors your iOS device seamlessly. Your contacts will be in place, your photos organized, and your apps ready to use. Smart Switch ensures that the transition is not just efficient but also preserves the continuity of your digital experience.

Making the switch to the Galaxy S24 Series becomes a stress-free endeavor with Smart Switch, allowing you to enjoy your new device without the worry of data loss or inconvenience.

Chapter 7:
Connectivity and Sharing

The Galaxy Connected Experience is a paradigm shift in the way we interact with technology, offering a seamless integration that goes beyond the capabilities of individual devices. It's about creating a harmonious ecosystem where your Galaxy S24 becomes a central hub, connecting and enhancing the functionality of your entire digital world.

With Galaxy Connected Experience, the boundaries between your devices dissolve, creating a unified ecosystem where your Galaxy S24 seamlessly communicates with other compatible Samsung devices. Whether it's a Galaxy Tab, a Galaxy Watch, or a Galaxy Book, the connectivity is designed to be intuitive and seamless.

Imagine starting a task on your Galaxy S24 and effortlessly transitioning to a larger screen on your Galaxy Book, or receiving calls and notifications on your Galaxy Watch. The interconnectedness of devices allows for smooth collaboration, enhancing productivity and providing a continuous experience.

Sharing files between your Galaxy devices has never been easier. Quick Share enables instant file transfers between Galaxy S24 and other Samsung devices with a simple tap. Whether it's a photo, video, or document, you can seamlessly send and receive files, eliminating the need for third-party apps or complicated processes.

Switching between devices becomes a fluid experience with the Galaxy Connected Experience. Imagine starting an email on your Galaxy Book, continuing it on your Galaxy S24 during your commute, and finalizing it on your Galaxy Tab over a cup of coffee—all without missing a beat.

The interconnected nature of the Galaxy Connected Experience doesn't compromise on security. Samsung Knox ensures that your data remains protected across all devices, providing a secure and seamless integration that enhances both efficiency and peace of mind.

As technology evolves, so does the Galaxy Connected Experience. Samsung is committed to providing regular updates and innovations to ensure that your devices stay seamlessly connected and that your digital experience continues to evolve with the latest advancements.

In essence, the Galaxy Connected Experience transforms the way we engage with our devices, fostering a connected, cohesive, and intuitive ecosystem that enhances every aspect of our digital lives.

Quick Share: Effortless sharing of photos, videos, and files

Quick Share is the epitome of seamless file sharing, designed to make the exchange of photos, videos, and various files among your Galaxy devices a breeze. With Quick Share, the days of searching for cables or relying on third-party apps are over; it's all about effortless and instantaneous sharing within your Galaxy ecosystem.

Key Features:

1. *Tap and Share:*
- Quick Share operates on a simple premise—tap and share. No need to navigate through multiple menus or set up complex configurations.
- A quick tap on the Quick Share icon, and your Galaxy S24 instantly identifies nearby compatible devices.

2. *Intuitive Device Selection:*
- Once activated, Quick Share displays a list of nearby Galaxy devices. It's a

visually intuitive process, allowing you to select the target device with a glance.

3. Multi-File Support:

- Quick Share isn't limited to a single file type. Whether it's a high-resolution photo, a 4K video, or a document, Quick Share ensures a swift and reliable transfer.

4. No Internet Required:

- Forget about relying on internet connectivity or cloud services. Quick Share functions through direct device-to-device communication, ensuring a fast and secure transfer regardless of your location.

5. *Receive with Ease:*

- On the receiving end, the process is equally straightforward. A notification prompts you to accept the incoming file, and with a tap, it seamlessly integrates into your device.

Use Cases:

1. *Sharing Memories:* Quickly share photos and videos from a gathering or an event with friends who are present, eliminating the need for group chats or email attachments.

2. *Collaborative Work:* In a collaborative work environment, easily share documents, presentations, or

project files during meetings without the hassle of connecting cables.

3. **Device Upgrade:** Transitioning to a new Galaxy device is smoother than ever. Use Quick Share to effortlessly transfer your apps, settings, and files from your old device to your new Galaxy S24.

4. **Spontaneous Sharing:** See an interesting article, webpage, or app? Share it instantly with friends who have compatible Galaxy devices.

Quick Share prioritizes security and privacy. The direct device-to-device transfer ensures that your files remain within your trusted Galaxy ecosystem, minimizing the risks associated with cloud-based transfers.

In essence, Quick Share embodies the essence of effortless and secure file sharing, redefining how we exchange content between our Galaxy devices.

Enhanced security with Knox and multi-device security

Security is a paramount concern in the digital age, and with the Galaxy S24 Series, Samsung has once again raised the bar by incorporating the robust Knox security platform and a comprehensive multi-device security approach. These features work seamlessly to safeguard your data, privacy, and overall peace of mind.

Knox Security Platform:

1. ***Defense-Grade Security:*** Knox is renowned for providing defense-grade security, and with the Galaxy S24, it's no different. It's a multi-layered platform designed to protect your device from the moment it boots up, offering real-time protection against malware, malicious threats, and unauthorized access.

2. ***Secure Boot Process:*** Knox ensures a secure boot process, verifying the integrity of the device's software at every step. This prevents the loading of unauthorized or tampered software, establishing a secure foundation for the entire system.

3. *Secure Folder:* For added security, the Galaxy S24 includes the Secure Folder feature. This encrypted space allows you to store sensitive files, apps, and data, providing an additional layer of protection that's separate from the regular device environment.

4. *Biometric Authentication:* Knox leverages advanced biometric authentication methods, such as fingerprint scanning and facial recognition, to ensure that only authorized users can access sensitive information on the device.

Multi-Device Security:

1. *Connected Ecosystem Security:* The
   Galaxy S24 extends its security umbrella
   beyond the device itself, embracing a
   multi-device security approach. This
   ensures that your data remains secure,
   whether you're using your smartphone,
   tablet, or other connected Galaxy devices.

2. *Secure Data Sharing:* Multi-device
   security encompasses secure data sharing
   among connected devices. Whether
   you're transferring files through Quick
   Share or accessing data across your
   Galaxy ecosystem, the emphasis on
   security remains unwavering.

3. Secure Communication: Knox ensures that communication between your Galaxy devices is encrypted and secure. This is particularly crucial for functions like Live Translate, where real-time language translations take place over calls or texts.

4. Privacy Controls: The Galaxy S24 empowers users with robust privacy controls. From managing app permissions to controlling access to sensitive data, these controls provide users with the ability to customize their privacy settings according to their preferences.

In conclusion, the combination of the Knox Security Platform and multi-device security measures elevates the Galaxy S24 Series to new heights in terms of ensuring the privacy and security of its users. Whether you're an individual user or a business professional, these features offer peace of mind in an increasingly interconnected world.

Sustainability initiatives and commitment to a greener future

Samsung, with the Galaxy S24 Series, is committed to making meaningful contributions to environmental preservation and reducing the ecological footprint. The company believes in the power of small changes, and through various initiatives, aims to build a sustainable path for the future.

1. Sustainable Materials: The Galaxy S24 Series is crafted with a focus on sustainable materials. Samsung is committed to reducing its reliance on non-renewable resources and integrating eco-friendly materials in the manufacturing process. This includes the use of recycled and responsibly sourced materials, contributing to a more circular and sustainable product lifecycle.

2. Recycling Programs: Samsung actively promotes recycling initiatives to reduce electronic waste. Through strategic partnerships and recycling programs, the company encourages users to responsibly dispose of their old devices. This ensures that electronic components are properly recycled, minimizing environmental impact.

3. Energy Efficiency: The Galaxy S24 Series incorporates energy-efficient technologies to reduce overall energy consumption. From optimized processors to intelligent battery management, these features not only enhance user experience but also contribute to a more energy-efficient usage pattern.

4. E-Waste Reduction: Samsung is dedicated to reducing electronic waste by designing products with longevity in mind. The Galaxy S24 Series is built to withstand the test of time, reducing the frequency of device replacements. This not only benefits users economically but also contributes to the reduction of electronic waste.

5. Sustainable Packaging: The packaging of the Galaxy S24 Series is designed with sustainability in mind. Samsung is committed to minimizing packaging waste by using recycled and eco-friendly materials. Additionally, the company continues to explore innovative packaging solutions that are both functional and environmentally responsible.

6. Carbon Neutrality: Samsung is actively working towards achieving carbon neutrality across its operations. This includes efforts to reduce carbon emissions during the manufacturing process and throughout the product lifecycle. The Galaxy S24 Series aligns with these sustainability goals, contributing to a lower carbon footprint.

7. Environmental Certifications: The Galaxy S24 Series adheres to various environmental certifications and standards. These certifications validate Samsung's commitment to meeting stringent environmental criteria, ensuring that the devices are produced with the least environmental impact possible.

In summary, the Galaxy S24 Series stands as a testament to Samsung's commitment to sustainability. By incorporating eco-friendly practices, reducing electronic waste, and embracing a circular economy approach, Samsung is taking significant strides towards creating a greener and more sustainable future. The Galaxy S24 Series exemplifies the harmonious coexistence of cutting-edge technology and environmental responsibility.

Chapter 8:

Storage, Trade-In, and Accessories

The Galaxy S24 Series offers users a versatile range of storage options to cater to diverse needs and preferences. With choices ranging from 128GB, 256GB, to a capacious 512GB, Samsung ensures that users have the flexibility to select the storage capacity that aligns with their usage patterns and requirements.

1. 128GB Storage: The 128GB storage option is perfect for users who prioritize a balance between affordability and sufficient storage space. It provides ample room for storing apps, photos, videos, and other essential data without compromising on performance.

2. 256GB Storage: For users who require more extensive storage for their multimedia content, applications, and files, the 256GB option offers a substantial upgrade. This variant is well-suited for individuals with a penchant for capturing high-resolution photos and videos or those who store a significant amount of data on their devices.

3. 512GB Storage: The 512GB storage option represents the pinnacle of storage capacity, catering to power users, professionals, and enthusiasts who demand extensive space for their digital content. This variant is ideal for those who store large media libraries, engage in resource-intensive tasks, or simply prefer the convenience of expansive storage.

These diverse storage options empower users to customize their Galaxy S24 experience based on their storage needs, ensuring that they have the freedom to utilize their smartphones to the fullest extent. Whether it's capturing precious moments, downloading applications, or storing important files, the Galaxy S24 Series provides a storage solution for every user, contributing to a seamless and personalized mobile experience.

Trade-in options for savings

In today's fast-paced technological landscape, staying up-to-date with the latest innovations is key to unlocking the full potential of your mobile experience. Recognizing the evolving needs of users, Samsung introduces convenient trade-in options for those eager to embrace the cutting-edge Galaxy S24 Series.

Trade-in programs offer users a seamless pathway to upgrade their devices while maximizing savings. Samsung's commitment to sustainability aligns with these initiatives, providing a responsible way to part ways with older devices. This not only reduces electronic waste but also contributes to a more sustainable and eco-friendly tech ecosystem.

How It Works:

The process is designed to be user-friendly and efficient. Users can initiate the trade-in process by visiting the official Samsung website or authorized retail partners. The website typically features a dedicated section for trade-ins, guiding users through the steps to evaluate their device's trade-in value.

While the specific criteria may vary, trade-in programs generally consider factors such as the device's model, age, and overall condition. Devices in good condition typically fetch better trade-in values, offering users increased savings on their new Galaxy S24 or S24+.

Choosing to trade in an old device contributes significantly to environmental sustainability. Samsung ensures that traded-in devices are processed responsibly, with recycling programs aimed at minimizing electronic waste. This commitment aligns with Samsung's broader vision of fostering a circular economy within the tech industry.

Trade-in options not only make upgrading more affordable but also enhance the overall accessibility of cutting-edge technology. By offsetting the cost of the new Galaxy S24 or S24+, users can experience the latest features, innovations, and performance without a hefty price tag.

As users increasingly seek cost-effective and environmentally conscious choices, trade-in programs emerge as a win-win solution, allowing them to seamlessly transition to the Galaxy S24 Series while contributing to a more sustainable future.

Galaxy S24 and S24+ accessories

In the world of smartphones, the device is just the beginning of the journey. Samsung understands that accessorizing plays a crucial role in enhancing the overall mobile experience. With the launch of the Galaxy S24 Series, a range of thoughtfully crafted accessories is introduced, designed to complement and elevate the user experience.

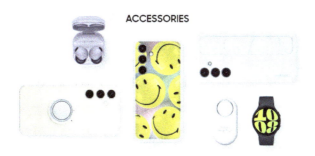

For those who prioritize both style and functionality, the Silicone Case in Yellow offers a vibrant and durable option. The case not only adds a pop of color to your Galaxy S24 but also provides a secure grip and protection against daily wear and tear. The sleek design ensures that your device remains comfortably pocketable while making a bold fashion statement.

Tech enthusiasts who appreciate the sleek aesthetics of their Galaxy S24 or S24+ can opt for the Clear Gadget Case. This minimalist accessory allows the phone's design to shine through while providing essential protection against scratches and minor impacts. The clear case effortlessly complements the device's unified design philosophy, showcasing its satin finish and refined curves.

Embrace the convenience of wireless charging with the specially designed Wireless Charging Pad. This accessory eliminates the hassle of cables and connectors, allowing users to charge their Galaxy S24 or S24+ effortlessly. The pad's compact and stylish design makes it a perfect addition to your workspace or bedside table, ensuring that your device stays charged and ready whenever you need it.

For those who value a combination of sophistication and functionality, the Leather Wallet Cover is an ideal choice. Crafted from premium materials, this accessory not only protects your Galaxy S24 but also serves as a practical wallet with card slots and a cash pocket. The leather finish adds a touch of luxury, making it a perfect companion for both professional and casual settings.

Complete your immersive Galaxy experience with the Galaxy Buds Pro. These wireless earbuds deliver superior sound quality, intelligent active noise cancellation, and a comfortable fit. Whether you're on a call, listening to music, or catching up on podcasts, the Galaxy Buds Pro seamlessly integrate with your Galaxy S24 or S24+, providing an audio experience that matches the device's performance.

Combine style with functionality using the Smart LED View Cover. This innovative accessory not only protects your Galaxy S24 or S24+ but also features a smart LED display on the cover. Get at-a-glance notifications, check the time, and even answer calls without opening the cover. The LED icons add a touch of futuristic flair to your device.

Samsung's commitment to providing a holistic mobile experience is reflected in the diverse range of accessories available for the Galaxy S24 Series. Whether it's about protection, convenience, or style, these accessories cater to a variety of user preferences, ensuring that your Galaxy S24 or S24+ is not just a device but a personalized and versatile companion.

Conclusion

As we conclude this journey through the groundbreaking Galaxy S24 Series, it's essential to recap the key highlights that make these devices truly exceptional. Samsung has once again pushed the boundaries of innovation, seamlessly blending cutting-edge technology, captivating design, and unparalleled camera features.

The Galaxy S24 and S24+ stand as a testament to Samsung's commitment to delivering a superior mobile experience. From the expansive display and enhanced battery life to the innovative camera system and the introduction of Galaxy AI, every aspect has been meticulously crafted to redefine what users can expect from a smartphone.

The unified design philosophy, featuring a satin finish and fortified with Armor Aluminum, not only adds durability but also elevates the aesthetic appeal of the devices. The extensive color palette, including exclusive options, allows users to express their style and individuality.

The integration of Galaxy AI brings forth a new era of possibilities, from real-time language translation with Live Translate to intuitive search experiences with Circle to Search. The ProVisual engine enhances photography, ensuring that every shot is a masterpiece, even in low-light conditions.

To the readers who are now proud owners of the Galaxy S24 Series, this is an invitation to explore the full potential of your device. Dive into the seamless multitasking facilitated by Galaxy AI, capture moments with Nightography, and embrace the joy of gaming with the larger Vapor Chamber. The Galaxy S24 Series is not just a smartphone; it's a companion that adapts to your lifestyle, making every interaction effortless and enjoyable.

In the intersection of innovation, design, and camera mastery, the Galaxy S24 Series emerges as a pinnacle of technological achievement. It's not merely about owning a smartphone; it's about possessing a tool that empowers and inspires. As technology continues to evolve, Samsung remains at the forefront, shaping the future of mobile experiences.

As you embark on this journey with your Galaxy S24 or S24+, remember that the true essence lies not just in the features listed on paper but in the moments you capture, the tasks you accomplish, and the seamless integration of technology into your daily life. The Galaxy S24 Series is not just a device; it's an enabler of possibilities, a conduit to creativity, and a companion in your pursuit of excellence.

In your hands, the Galaxy S24 Series is more than a smartphone; it's a gateway to a world of endless potential. Embrace the future, explore the capabilities, and let the Galaxy S24 Series be your partner in this exhilarating technological voyage.

www.ingramcontent.com/pod-product-compliance
Lightning Source LLC
LaVergne TN
LVHW051735050326
832903LV00023B/929